Share Time

HOUGHTON MIFFLIN HARCOURT

School Publishers

Contents

Ann Packs

by Ellen Catala

illustrated by Diane Paterson

"I miss Ann. I can call Ann.
Ann can come here," said Nan.

"Yes," said Ann. "I will come.
I will be quick, Nan."

4

Quick, quick, quick!
Ann will pack a big red bag.

Ann will pack ten hats.
Ann will pack ten socks.
Pack, pack, pack, pack.

Ann will pack six ducks.
Ann will pack ten dolls.
Pack, pack, pack, pack.

Ann has hats and socks.
Ann has ducks and dolls.
Ann has ten big hugs for Nan.

Tess and Jack

by Timothy Bern

illustrated by Marsha Winborn

"Call me," said Tess.
"Call me," said Jack.

Tess is sick. Tess is sick in bed.
Tess cannot play, but Tess can
call Jack.

Jack is sick. Jack is sick in bed.
Jack cannot play, but Jack can
call Tess.

Tess is well. Tess is back. Tess
can play. Jack is well. Jack is
back. Jack can play. Tess and
Jack can bat.

Will Jack call Tess?
Yes! Yes! Jack will.
Will Tess call Jack?
Yes! Yes! Tess will.

Tess has a mitt.

Jack has his bat.

"Quick!" said Tess. "Hit it

Tess and Jack had fun!

A Duck in Mud

by Deborah Jensen

illustrated by Bob Barner

Duck is in mud. Yuck!

Duck has to get help!
Duck quacks, "Red Hen!
Quick! Come get me!"

"Look at the mess I am in,"
Duck quacks. "I am in mud!"

"I will get Mack!" yells Red Hen.
"Get back quick," Duck quacks.

18

Red Hen is back with Mack.

Mack tugs. Tug, tug. TUG!

Mack did it!
Duck is not in mud.
Duck can get away!

Ducks Quack

by Kyle Stenovich

Look up at the ducks.

Quack, quack, quack.

Hear the ducks quack.

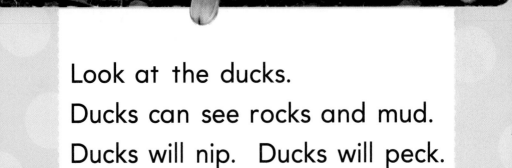

Look at the ducks.

Ducks can see rocks and mud.

Ducks will nip. Ducks will peck.

Ducks will go in.
Ducks will get wet.
Ducks will quack.
Quack, quack, quack.

Look at the ducks.

Ducks will dip in.

Dip, dip, dip.

Ducks will pop back up.
Pop, pop, pop.

Hear the duck on the hill.
Every duck can quack.
Quack, quack, quack.

Brad and Cris

by Teresa Bashin

illustrated by Marsha Winborn

Brad Frog is red. Brad has tan
dots. Brad is red and tan.

Brad has a pal. His pal is Cris.
Cris Frog is tan. Cris has no
dots. Cris is tan and red.

"We will go on a trip, Cris,"
Brad said. "It will be fun."
Brad did not tell Cris why.

Brad led Cris. Brad and Cris
hop on pads. Hop, hop! Hop,
hop, hop!

"Can we get some bugs and
grubs?" said Cris.
"Not yet," said Brad. "Not yet."

"Look, Brad!" Cris said. "Bugs,
bugs, bugs! Grubs, grubs, grubs!
Yum!"

What Did Dad Get?

by Ed Floyd
illustrated by Julia Gorton

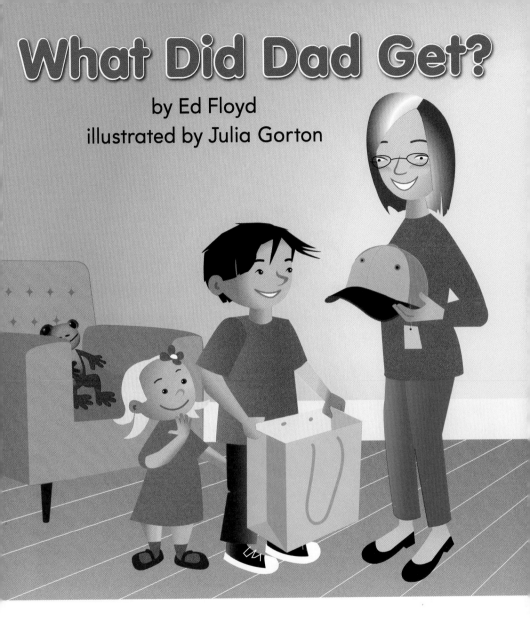

Fred has a big bag. Gram has a tan cap. It is for Dad.

Fred can hold up the bag. Gram
will drop the tan cap in it. Pop!

Jill can get the bag. Jill has an
animal. It is a red frog!

Pop! Jill drops the red frog in the
bag. It is for Dad.

"Gram," said Fred, "Dad has a
red frog. How did Dad get it?"

Dad has his tan cap. Dad has a
red frog on top of his cap. Fred,
Jill, and Gram grin at Dad.

Crabs

by Carlos Miranda

This is a crab.
It is a big, big crab.

A crab has ten legs.
Yes! A crab has ten legs!

Crabs zip on wet rocks.
Crabs sit on wet rocks.
Crabs like wet rocks!

Crabs can grip and grab.
Do not pick up a crab.
A crab can grab you!

Crabs can make tracks.
Crab tracks can zig.
Crab tracks can zag.

It is fun to look at crabs.
It is lots of fun!

The Big Job

by Pamela Chin

illustrated by John Ceballos

Dad has a job. Dad will go to his
job. Sid has a job. Sid will go to
his job.

Dad has a big red truck.
Dad will lug bricks in his truck.

Sid has a red truck. Sid will drop
his bricks on the grass.

Dad will dig up lots of rocks.
Dig, dig, dig, Dad!

Sid will dig up lots of rocks.
Dig, dig, dig, Sid!

Dad is back with Sid.
Why will Sid sit with Dad?
Dad and Sid will play!

Our Flag
by Susan Crowton

Up, up, up. The flag is on top.
It can flap. It can flip.

Up, up, up. The flag is on top.
It can flip. It can flap.

Our club has a big flag. We will sing. We will clap.

The flag is big. It is flat. They hold it up, up, up. They will not let it drop.

Flags can flip. Flags can flap.
Kids hold flags up, up, up.
Flags flap. Flags flip.

Flags, flags, flags. Pam has a flag. She is glad she has it.

The Plan

by Martin Avalong
illustrated by Linda Bronson

Hen has a plan. Cluck, cluck,
cluck. Hen will tell it to Duck.
Run, Hen! Run, run!

Did Duck like her plan? Yes, yes, yes! Duck flaps, flaps, flaps. Duck claps, claps, claps. Hen and Duck will play today.

Duck and Hen will have fun. Hen
trips, slips, and flips. Duck will,
too. Trip, trip, trip! Slip, slip, slip!
Flip, flip, flip!

Hen claps, flaps, and slaps. Duck
will, too. Clap, flap, slap!

Hen flops, clops, and plops. Duck
will, too. Flop, clop, plop!

Hen quits. Duck quits. Hen had a
good plan. Now it is good to sit.
Sit, sit, sit!

Our Sled Club

by Beatrice Wolfe

illustrated by Sonja Lamut

Our club is a sled club.
Our sled club has a plan.

Glen has a tan sled.
Glen tugs his tan sled
up Block Hill.

Roz has a black sled.
Roz tugs her black sled
up, up Block Hill.

Dan has a red sled.
Dan tugs his red sled
up, up, up Block Hill.

Glen yells, "Hop on!"
Roz yells, "Get set!"
Now Dan yells, "Go!"

We grip our sleds.
We will not flip.
We will not flop.
Our Sled Club has fun!

The Pet Club

by Ellen Catala

illustrated by Molly Delaney

Would you like to see pets?
Come to The Pet Club.

Dom has a pet. His pet is Ham.
Ham can flip. Ham can flop.

Roz has a pet cat. Her pet is
Glenn. Glenn can kick.

Todd has a pet dog. His pet is
Slim. Slim can run. Slim can sit.

Ann has a pet. Her pet is Bluff.
Bluff can clack. Bluff can flap.

Nick has a pet. His pet is Plum.
Plum will not flip, flop, and clack.
Plum will not play, but Plum will kiss!

Step Up!

by Tanya Rivers

The clock struck 8.

We go to the bus stop.

Step up! Step up!

Can Jess read? Yes, Jess can!
Can Stan read? Yes, Stan can!

Kim can write A, B, C.
Kim can spell.

Jill will snap blocks.
Jill will snap stacks and stacks.

We pick a good spot.
Peg will spin. Bess will spin.
Jen will spin.

Is it fun to step, step, step?
Is it fun to skip and sing?
Yes, it is! It is fun, fun, fun!

Splat! Splat!

by Svetlana Yarmey
illustrated by Rusty Fletcher

Meg has on a red smock.
Stan has on a tan smock.

Splat! Splat! Meg will draw
spots. Meg will draw dots.
What good pictures Meg has!

Snip! Snap! Stan will snip scraps.
Stan will snap blocks. What good
trucks Stan has!

Yum! Yum! Mom has snacks.
Stan will stop for a snack. Stan
has a big snack.

Stan has his snack. Yum! Yum!
Will Meg stop for a snack? Will
Meg skip her snack?

Meg will skip it.
Splat! Splat! Splat!

Nuts for Ben and Jen

by Sam Sussman

illustrated by Diane Blasirs

Ben likes to draw pictures.
Jen cuts strips. Snip, snip!
It is fun.

Sniff, sniff, sniff. Ben smells nuts.
Yum! Snacks!
Ben runs up after the smell.

Sniff, sniff, sniff. Jen smells nuts.

Yum! Snacks!

Jen runs down after the smell.

Are snacks in the red box?

Jen picks it up.

The lid is stuck.

Ben runs to help Jen.

Ben gets a stick.

Up pops the lid.

Snap! Snap! Snap!
Ben gets ten nuts. Yum!
Snap! Snap! Snap!
Jen gets ten nuts. Yum!

Miss Tess Was Still

by Ted Lutgen

illustrated by Mircea Catusanu

Miss Tess was still. Miss Tess was as still as a stick.

Now Miss Tess will skip.
Skip! Skip! Skip!

Miss Tess will do a split.
Split! Split! Split!

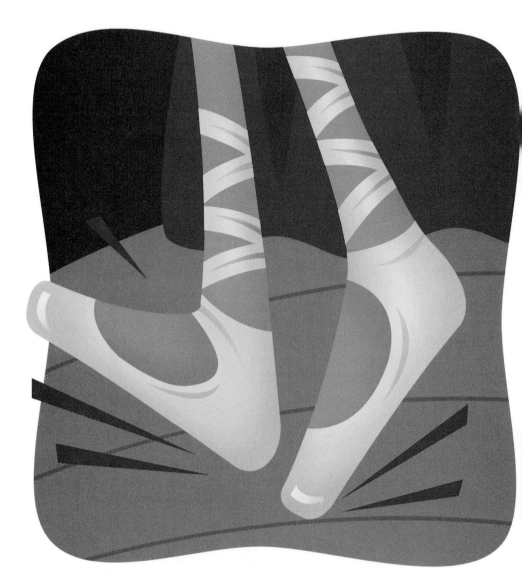

Miss Tess will step and tap.
Step! Step! Tap! Tap! Tap!

Miss Tess will spin. Miss Tess will
spin like a top. Spin! Spin! Spin!

Miss Tess has to stop. Miss Tess
will be still. Miss Tess will grin.
Click! Click! Click!

Who Likes to Jump?

by Cyrus Rivera

It is fun to jump. Gus and Liz
went to play. Gus and Liz run
and jump on a sand hill.

Fran will hop, jump, and land
on 7. Next, Fran will hop, jump,
and land on 8 and 9.

Jill will grasp the ends with her hands. Jill will jump as fast as she can. Jump, jump, jump!

Russ must jump and hit. Russ can
jump up, up, up. Russ can hit.
Russ can jump and hit.

Len is on a track. Len will run like the wind. Len will bend his legs and jump, jump, jump.

It is fun to take small jumps and
big jumps. Jump, jump, jump!

The Lost Cat

by Jane Nicholas
illustrated by Kristen Goeters

"Mick!" said Bess. "Muff is lost!
Ask Trent to help us."

Trent is at his desk.

"Muff is lost? Yes! Yes! I will help,"
said Trent. "We must find Muff!"

Trent plans his task.

"Hunt," Trent said. "We must hunt and hunt and hunt."

"Here is one hint. Cat tracks!
Tracks can take us to Muff."

Trent went past the plant stand.
At last, Trent can see Muff.

Muff is not lost! Muff has small
kits. Muff and her kits will rest
and rest.

Flint and Scamp

by Joe Capalletti

illustrated by Deborah Borgo

Camp is fun for Flint and Scamp.

Flint and Scamp run.

Flint and Scamp jump.

Camp is at an end.
Flint will miss Scamp.
Scamp will miss Flint.

Flint will write to Scamp.

Flint must get a stamp.

Gramps will give him one.

Scamp will write to Flint.

Scamp must get a stamp.

Gramps will give him one.

A big gust of wind comes.
Flint must run fast.
Scamp must run fast.

Flint and Scamp sit and read.
Flint and Scamp have fun!

The List

by Ellen Catala

illustrated by Dorothy Donahue

"Take this list," Mom tells Brent.
"Run and get what is on the list."

Brent runs fast. Brent runs
too fast! He drops his list.

Brent is at the stand. Brent hunts
and hunts, but his list is lost.

Brent gets stamps, eggs, and buns. Brent gets nuts and mints.

Brent put the sack on his back.
Brent did not stop to eat a snack.

"I lost the list," Brent tells Mom,
"but I got stamps, eggs, buns,
nuts, and mints."
"Brent is the best!" said Mom.

Word Lists

Accompanies
"Jack and the Wolf"

Ann Packs
page 3

Decodable Words
Target Skill: Short *a*
Ann, bag, can, has, hats, Nan, pack

Target Skills: Double Final Consonants
and *ck*
Ann, dolls, ducks, miss, pack, quick,
socks, will

Previously Taught Skills
big, hugs, red, six, ten, yes

High-Frequency Words
New
call, come, said

Previously Taught
a, and, be, for, here, I

Tess and Jack
page 9

Decodable Words
Target Skill: Short *a*
back, bat, can, cannot, had, has, Jack

Target Skills: Double Final Consonants
and *ck*
back, Jack, mitt, quick, sick, Tess, well,
will

Previously Taught Skills
bed, but, fun, his, hit, in, is, it, yes

High-Frequency Words
New
call, said

Previously Taught
a, and, me, play

A Duck in Mud

page 15

Decodable Words
Target Skill: Short *a*
am, at, back, can, has, Mack, quacks

Target Skills: Double Final Consonants
and *ck*
back, Duck, Mack, mess, quacks, quick, will, yells, yuck

Previously Taught Skills
did, get, Hen, in, is, it, mud, not, Red, tug, tugs

High-Frequency Words
New
away, come

Previously Taught
help, I, look, me, the, to, with

Ducks Quack

page 21

Decodable Words
Target Skill: Short *a*
at, back, can, quack

Target Skills: Double Final Consonants
and *ck*
back, duck, ducks, hill, peck, quack, rocks, will

Previously Taught Skills
dip, get, in, mud, nip, on, pop, up, wet

High-Frequency Words
New
every, hear

Previously Taught
and, go, look, see, the

Brad and Cris

page 27

Decodable Words
Target Skill: Short *i*
Cris, did, his, is, it, trip, will

Target Skill: Clusters with *r*
Brad, Cris, Frog, grubs, trip

Previously Taught Skills
bugs, can, dots, fun, get, has, hop, led, not, on, pads, pal, red, tan, tell, yet, yum

High-Frequency Words
New
some, why

Previously Taught
a, and, be, go, look, no, said, we

What Did Dad Get?

page 33

Decodable Words
Target Skill: Short *i*
big, did, grin, his, in, is, it, Jill, will

Target Skill: Clusters with *r*
drop, drops, Fred, frog, Gram, grin

Previously Taught Skills
an, at, bag, can, cap, Dad, get, has, on, pop, red, tan, top, up

High-Frequency Words
New
animal, how, of

Previously Taught
a, and, for, hold, said, the, what

Crabs
page 39

Decodable Words
Target Skill: Short *i*
big, grip, is, it, pick, sit, zig, zip

Target Skill: Clusters with *r*
crab, crabs, grab, grip, tracks

Previously Taught Skills
at, can, fun, has, legs, lots, not, on,
rocks, ten, up, wet, yes, zag

High-Frequency Words
New
make, of

Previously Taught
a, and, do, like, look, to, you

The Big Job
page 45

Decodable Words
Target Skill: Short *i*
big, bricks, dig, his, in, is, Sid, sit, will

Target Skill: Clusters with *r*
bricks, drop, grass, truck

Previously Taught Skills
back, Dad, has, job, lots, lug, red, rocks,
on, up

High-Frequency Words
New
of, why

Previously Taught
a, and, go, play, the, to, with

Our Flag

Decodable Words
Target Skill: Short *o*
drop, not, on, top

Target Skill: Clusters with *l*
clap, club, flag, flags, flap, flat, flip, glad

Previously Taught Skills
big, can, has, is, it, kids, let, Pam, up, will

High-Frequency Words
New
our, she

Previously Taught
a, hold, sing, the, they, we

The Plan

Decodable Words
Target Skill: Short *o*
clop, clops, flop, flops, plop, plops

Target Skill: Clusters with *l*
clap, claps, clop, clops, cluck, flap, flaps,
flip, flips, flop, flops, plan, plop, plops,
slap, slaps, slip, slips

Previously Taught Skills
did, Duck, fun, had, has, Hen, is, it,
quits, run, sit, tell, trip, trips, will, yes

High-Frequency Words
New
her, now, today

Previously Taught
a, and, good, have, like,
play, to, too

Our Sled Club

page 63

Decodable Words
Target Skill: Short *o*
Block, flop, hop, not, on, Roz

Target Skill: Clusters with *l*
black, Block, club, flip, flop, Glen, plan, sled, sleds

Words with Previously Taught Skills
Dan, fun, get, grip, has, Hill, his, is, red, set, tan, tugs, up, will, yells

High-Frequency Words
New
her, now, our

Previously Taught
a, go, we

The Pet Club

page 69

Decodable Words
Target Skill: Short *o*
dog, Dom, flop, not, Roz, Todd

Target Skill: Clusters with *l*
Bluff, clack, club, flap, flip, flop, Glenn, Plum, Slim

Previously Taught Skills
Ann, but, can, cat, Ham, has, his, is, kick, kiss, Nick, pet, pets, run, sit, will

High-Frequency Words
New
her, would

Previously Taught
a, and, come, like, play, see, the, to, you

128

Accompanies
"Dr. Seuss"

Step Up!

page 75

Decodable Words
Target Skill: Short *e*
Bess, Jen, Jess, Peg, spell, step, yes

Target Skill: Clusters with *s*
skip, snap, spell, spin, spot, stacks,
Stan, step, stop, struck

Previously Taught Skills
8, A, B, C, blocks, bus, can, clock, fun,
is, it, Jill, Kim, pick, up, will

High-Frequency Words
New
read, write

Previously Taught
a, and, go, good, sing, the,
to, we

Splat! Splat!

page 81

Decodable Words
Target Skill: Short *e*
Meg, red

Target Skill: Clusters with *s*
scraps, skip, smock, snack, snacks,
snap, snip, splat, spots, Stan, stop

Previously Taught Skills
big, blocks, dots, has, his, it, Mom, on,
tan, trucks, will, yum

High-Frequency Words
New
draw, pictures

Previously Taught
a, for, good, her, what

129

Nuts for Ben and Jen

page 87

Decodable Words
Target Skill: Short *e*
Ben, gets, Jen, red, smell, smells, ten

Target Skill: Clusters with *s*
smell, smells, snacks, snap, sniff, snip,
stick, strips, stuck

Words with Previously Taught Skills
box, cuts, fun, in, is, it, lid, nuts, picks,
pops, runs, up, yum

High-Frequency Words
New
after, draw, pictures

Previously Taught
a, are, help, likes,
the, to

Miss Tess Was Still

page 93

Decodable Words
Target Skill: Short *e*
Tess, step

Target Skill: Clusters with *s*
skip, spin, split, step, stick, still, stop

Previously Taught Skills
as, click, grin, has, Miss, tap, top, will

High-Frequency Words
New
was

Previously Taught
a, and, be, do, like, now, to

Who Likes to Jump?

page 99

Decodable Words
Target Skill: Short *u*
fun, Gus, jump, jumps, must, run, Russ, up

Target Skill: Final Clusters
and, bend, ends, fast, grasp, hands, jump, jumps, land, must, sand, went, wind

Previously Taught Skills
7, 8, 9, as, big, can, Fran, hill, his, hit, hop, is, it, Jill, legs, Len, Liz, on, track, will

High-Frequency Words
New
small, take

Previously Taught
a, her, like, play, she, the, to, with

The Lost Cat

page 105

Decodable Words
Target Skill: Short *u*
hunt, Muff, must, us

Target Skill: Final Clusters
and, ask, desk, help, hint, hunt, last, lost, must, past, plant, rest, stand, task, Trent, went

Previously Taught Skills
at, Bess, can, cat, has, his, is, kits, Mick, not, plans, tracks, will, yes

High-Frequency Words
New
one, small, take

Previously Taught
find, her, here, I, said, see, the, to, we

Flint and Scamp

page 111

Decodable Words
Target Skill: Short *u*
fun, gust, jump, must, run

Target Skill: Final Clusters
and, camp, end, fast, Flint, Gramps,
gust, jump, must, Scamp, stamp, wind

Previously Taught Skills
an, at, big, get, him, is, miss, sit, will

High-Frequency Words
New
give, one

Previously Taught
a, comes, for, have, of, read,
to, write

The List

page 117

Decodable Words
Target Skill: Short *u*
buns, but, hunts, nuts, run, runs

Target Skill: Final Clusters
and, best, Brent, fast, hunts, list, lost,
mints, stamps, stand

Previously Taught Skills
at, back, did, drops, eggs, get, gets, got,
his, is, Mom, not, on, sack, snack, stop,
tells

High-Frequency Words
New
eat, put, take

Previously Taught
a, he, I, said, the, to, too,
what